Mask Of A Man

Being Married To A Name

Ebonie Clayton

Copyright© 2021

All Rights Reserved

Table of Contents

Dedication	i
Acknowledgments	ii
About The Author	iii
Chapter 1: Blurred Expectations	1
Chapter 2: The Break Up	16
Chapter 3: New Beginnings	32
Chapter 4: The Kids	39
Chapter 5: Time For Change	45

Dedication

I would like to dedicate this to men and women that deal with emotional, mental, and psychological abuse.

Encourage them to heal and let their story continue after the breakup and removal of the thing causing them pain.

Encourage them to let the light fill the dark places they have inside. That the abuser saw the light they never saw and only wanted to shine in their place.

Acknowledgments

God, my family, my kids, Tiffany Buckner, and all who worked on this for me and with me.

About The Author

Ebonie Clayton is a black woman from South Georgia. A small town called Adel. She played many sports including softball, basketball, and tennis growing up but instead of continuing with sports she stopped after high school and moved to Atlanta, GA, for two years of college for her prerequisites for nursing at Clayton State University. Then she moved back down south and completed her nursing degree at ABAC College. She got married and divorced and birthed three beautiful babies during that time.

She loves being a mom. Their happiness is what drives her, along with God's grace and mercy and him being the head of their lives.

Chapter 1: Blurred Expectations

When it starts, you think about how cute this person is. How good they smell. How their lips feel. How the conversation seems to last forever. You blur out the facts and red flags. You also see others happy, and society tempts you to think you must find that happiness quickly. And families, well, they say you gotta make sure you get a husband. All of these things combined make it harder to see true love and understanding with a person. To truly dive into the depths of the earth of a person and get the core values out of them is a difficult task that requires attention and dedication. So, to save time and effort, we accept surface qualities without probing deeper into the person and getting to know them.

When Bella met Wade, they became friends instantly. They would talk about everything, and that mostly had to do with his looks. He was so cute that she was okay with opening up to him. He had green eyes, a nice, tanned, chiseled body, and long, dark, curly hair. Bella would find this a real immature love looking back because his looks had her captivated, but it wasn't just that. Wade was very smart as well. Honor graduate in high school. He did not curse all the time, unlike many people Bella had come to know. He told Bella that, growing up, he would go to church with his great uncle each Sunday and spend time making cakes with his aunt and giving them to sick people. The family-oriented person Bella was growing up saw him as a perfect husband candidate. They were both young, but the potential to be something great was there.

Bella saw him first at her senior trip to Universal Studios in Florida. Bella was shy, but she was determined to put herself out there more in recent years, so she walked up to him and said hello. They started talking and decided to exchange numbers. Over the next month, she would not hear from him, and then randomly, she received a text from him saying, "Hello, gorgeous." Bella had been working a job leading up to her graduation and getting prepared for college. She planned to go to a college in Arkansas because she loved her family and did not want to be too far away from them, but after spending multiple nights on the phone with Wade, she changed her mind and wanted to go to school in Florida. Her family was against this, but with her life bottled up, Bella felt she needed to make her life her own by leaving the state and traveling and meeting new people, especially meeting back up with Wade. She loved animations and gaming, so she began searching for colleges in Florida and found The Dave School. She had talked with Wade about it, and he explained that he only lived twenty minutes from the school site. Bella planned a trip to visit the campus to decide if this was the school she wanted to go to. When she arrived with her family, she loved it. It was warm, and the atmosphere was more than what she could have hoped for. The guide took them on tour and made her familiar with different areas she would need if she decided to attend this institute. After this was complete, Bella's mind was made up. She wanted to go to school here, not only because she would be closer to Wade, but because it looked like everything she wanted from her educational institute. Her mother and father did not understand why she could not just go to a school in Arkansas, so they decided they would talk to her about it more at the hotel later that evening. They ordered some pizza and sat down by the pool to eat.

Dawn, her mother, asked, "Honey, how do you like it here?"

Bella said, "I love it, and I can't wait to start school. I mean, can you imagine going to the beach and doing my homework while listening to the waves in the evening?"

Her mother said, "Yes, I can imagine that would be nice, but there are nice places to do your studies back in Arkansas. Is it possible that you are leaving for this boy that you met when you came here?"

Bella said, "I mean, I would like to see how things could be with him, but this school is phenomenal as well."

Bernard, her dad, said, "Listen, don't come here for a relationship with a boy. You need to be sure this is not about that, or I will be sure not to help you with your school expenses when your grades drop because you stopped staying focused on your studies."

Bella became quite furious because she had kept her grades up her entire life, and never once was she allowed to make her own decisions or make mistakes without getting into trouble. When her father told her he wouldn't help her if she made a decision that went against his, she lost it. Bella stormed away. She called Wade and asked if he would come and get her for a little while. Wade said, "Sure, I'll be there in twenty minutes."

Wade and Bella talked for a while as he drove to meet her. Bella had explained that she thought her parents felt he would influence her negatively and that she just wanted to be able to see for herself. That she wishes they would just let her live her life. When Wade arrived, Bella got in the car.

Wade said, "I want your parents to meet me."

Bella was shocked. She did not expect him to want to meet with them. They had not, at this point, made anything official, so Bella could not understand why he would be willing to go to such lengths for her.

Bella tried to convince Wade that there was no need for that, but Wade insisted, saying, "I think this would be the most respectful thing to do."

Wade cut off the car and came over to Bella's side to open her car door. They walked to the pool area. Her parents were still sitting there. Wade opened the gate for her, and then he followed. Bella introduced Wade to her parents. Bernard stood up and shook his hand as Wade shook Dawn's hand as well. Wade said, "I just wanted to introduce myself and answer any questions you may have and try to alleviate any concerns you may have about me being a part of your daughter's life as her friend at this time." In Bella's mind, she was like, "What? Where did this man come from? He knows the right words to say, and he is not afraid of my dad."

She thought he must be the one for her. Bernard asked, "How old are you? Do you attend school, and do you work?"

Wade said, "I am twenty. I am not in college, but I do have my own business that I started right after I got out of high school putting in security systems."

Bella was shocked. He had never told her that. He had said to her that he worked but never what it was. Bella's dad was impressed. Dawn asked, "I just want to know what your intentions are with my daughter."

Wade said, "I intend to be her friend, but if a friend turns into something else, I still intend to be a gentleman with her and be her personal tour guide of Florida."

Bella laughed. She loved him. Already. Wade and Bella's family spent another few hours talking and getting to know each other. They called it a night, and Bella's parents began to walk back into the hotel. Bella tried to walk back out with Wade, but he said, "No, go with your family, so I know you make it to your room safely."

Bella said, "Okay, and thank you for everything," and gave him a kiss on the cheek. Wade gave her a smile and a head nod, and they parted ways. Bella went to bed that night knowing she would definitely come back, and as soon as Wade asked, he would be her man.

Bella moved to Florida. Her family was still worried, but they expressed that Wade seemed like an okay guy, but they told her to mainly remain focused on her studies and wished her the best. She arrived in Florida and ordered an Uber to campus. Bella was excited to start school and to meet up with Wade later. The fire between them had been heating up a bit since last seeing each other. When she arrived, she found her dorm room and started to unpack. After that, she called Wade. Wade again said that he would be right there. Bella thought, *I love that he works for himself and can come whenever I call or talk with me any time of the day.* Wade finally arrived and called to let her know that he was outside. Bella was surprised to see he had flowers for her and walked up to her and kissed her on the forehead. Bella fell into his arms and fell in love all over again. That night they made love for the first time, and Wade asked if they could make things official. Bella did not think twice about it and was more than excited and ready to make him her man.

Bella's parents raised her to be a hard worker. They did not raise her to depend on anyone for anything, so she didn't understand nor expect anyone to do anything for her. Therefore, her expectations were quite low, which allowed Wade to do minimal things to turn him from friend to boyfriend. He would bring flowers and her favorite snacks between classes and take her to dates at the beach for lunch. For Bella, it was a dream come true. He was so into her, or at least that's what she thought. She would constantly obsess over the littlest things about him. Her mind would only be filled with his thoughts. "O, you are so beautiful." "How could anyone want to be without you?" "Send me a picture of you." "Send me a new one every day of your beautiful face." "I want to see those beautiful eyes." "What's your favorite ice cream?" "I'll give you whatever you want just to see your face." "Even if it's just a few minutes on my break." "I have to see you." "I have to hold you." "You make me whole." "I love you." *Woah!*

The serenades of him never stopped in the beginning. It was all love, and it was all too quick. One night, while they were studying for a test she had, he insisted that they take a break to rest her mind. They turned on some music and danced around the room, but Bella was so clumsy she tripped. They both fell over onto the bed. They laughed jokingly, and he looked her in the eyes and said, "I love you."

Bella had been wondering when she would hear this from him, and hearing this from him confirmed that she was on the same page with him on the way she felt. She said, "I love you too, Wade." They began to kiss. Bella closed her eyes as Wade rubbed her skin softly. He left one hand on her love handle and rubbed the other hand up her back and into her hair. Bella looked at Wade and saw him looking back at her. He pulled her hair and made her head jerk back, and began kissing her on her neck. Bella felt like she was in a colorful tunnel of pure bliss. Wade began kissing her and went all the way down her body. His hands followed on her sides. The endorphins paralyzed Bella as the oxytocin made her limp. *There was no stopping this*, Bella thought happily. He pulled off her gray panties as Bella sat up to take off Wade's shirt. While taking it off, Wade's hair fell out of his ponytail. Bella looked at him, and her body instantly became ready for him. She loved the wild look he got when he was turned on. He took off his shorts as Bella kissed him all over his neck and chest and stomach. She was about to put him in her mouth, but he pulled away from her.

"I want you," he purred.

Bella laid back on the bed as he inched inside of her and handled her gently. They rolled around in different positions on the bed until it was almost close to climax.

Bella whispered, "I want to have your baby."

Wade replied, "Are you sure?"

"Yes."

"Okay."

He laid down on top of her and moaned her name. Then he pulled her close and came inside her. She groaned out of pleasure and let her head rest on the pillows. They held each other for the rest of the night.

The next morning Bella awoke late for her class. Wade was gone.

Bella wondered why he had not awakened her for her class. She got ready and hurried to her class. Alarms were ringing in her head, but she ignored them for sanity's sake. The instructor let Bella come in but with five points off her final grade. She took her test and headed to get some breakfast. Then she called Wade. Wade did not pick up. Bella thought it was weird because he almost always picked up the phone. She ate breakfast and went to her next class. After each class, Bella would check her phone with no call or text back from Wade. The day went by, and Wade didn't call until the next morning. When he did call, he chirped, "Hey, beautiful. I'm outside."

Bella rushed outside to meet with him. When she got there to let him in, she noticed he had a bag in his hand. He asked could she come outside instead. Bella, though a little worried by now, agreed. They sat in the car for a bit. Then Wade took out a Plan B.

"Here. You need to take this."

Bella was shocked.

She asked, "Why? I thought we were in love. We both wanted this."

Wade sighed. "Well, I was drunk the other night and not in the right state. I should not have done that. You got me so worked up when you fell on me in the room, and I just wanted to please you because you said you wanted a baby."

Bella thought to herself that she knew he had not been drinking with her all day. She was confused, but she did not want to make anyone be a dad that did not want to be."

Bella grabbed the water and pill. She swallowed the pill with a bitter taste in her mouth.

She could not speak for a while, but she knew she needed to say something. A small voice escaped her, "Do you still love me?"

He furrowed his brows. "Why would you ask me that? I show you that all the time. I'm always here for you, right? I don't need to prove my love for you just because I told you I cannot have a baby yet."

Bella realized that was rude, but she thought, *Maybe I did trap him into making that decision.*

He was always there for her, that was true, so she would not question his love for her and no longer ask for a baby. He was more important to her than a baby, and she would do anything to keep him in her life.

His words fluttered her heart. "Kiss me, kiss me, kiss me. Quick right here at the red light before I have to drive again. I just can't wait to have those lips on me, girl." He groaned.

Bella's heart and soul were into this man. She couldn't let him go. He called every day. He wanted to see how she was dressed. Asked her not to wear some things that were too tight and too short. He convinced Bella that she needed to save all of that for him, and eventually, she would only wear cute things around him. She would give herself excuses. Her blind love snubbed a small part of her that protested that he controlled her lifestyle. He was her boyfriend, she told herself. Who else did she need to be looking good for, right?

However, one day, it all came shattering down around her. Wade, the man she loved fiercely, suddenly decided he no longer wanted to be with her. It was all so sudden that Bella lost her bearings for a little while.

"I want to break up with you. I think I want to be with my old girlfriend. She is just better for me."

Click. Dial tone.

Wow.

Tears fell. Bella cried for hours. She didn't want to talk to anyone after it happened. She cut her phone off and didn't speak to her family for a few weeks. They ended up calling the room phone to talk with her in her dorm because they were worried about her. She lost a ton of weight from working out two hours a day and only eating a granola bar and yogurt once a day from depression.

She was sick but eventually started doing better. Bella blocked his number and tried to move forward with her life, but he messaged her on Facebook one day and asked if they could talk. He said his family had made him call and break things off with her because they liked his old girlfriend better. He also claimed he missed Bella too much to care what his family said anymore. He couldn't stand to be without her.

His words still held so much weight for her, and despite telling herself that she hated him and that she would never go back to him, she fell back in again. Like he never left. Her heart was all over him. Just wanting to give into him was too easy. This time she told him they could be friends, but only to read the Bible and pray together. He agreed, saying whatever he had to do to make it up to her. She thought it must be true love that brought him back, but it was all part of the game.

Bella and Wade stayed together for a while after that, with plenty more breakups and makeups and even a few Plan B's for the next year.

About two days before the beginning of summer, his ex-girlfriend had gotten Bella's phone number. She called her, talking about how she had been with him the entire time Wade was with Bella. She also told her they had slept together multiple times. Bella was so upset at this news that she slapped Wade when she saw him.

His audacity was ridiculous. He got angry and told her he did not want to do anything with her anymore. He canceled the plans for their upcoming summer trip, too. Bella felt bad and called him repeatedly. She left messages saying, "Please forgive me. I need you." Bella realized she would be better off without him, but the need for him was consuming her.

He called the morning of the trip, and they got back together right before. When they made it to the trip, coincidentally, his ex-girlfriend was there. Bella noticed that he had to leave many times throughout the trip, claiming he wanted some time alone. On the other hand, his ex-girlfriend claimed he had told her to come, and Bella thought she was merely disrespectful. In hindsight, however, she probably was telling the truth.

Bella and Wade were getting ready to leave for Florida, and the day before their departure, Bella almost fought his ex-girlfriend.

Wow!

She never had to fight anyone in her whole life. Everyone was always her friend. This day was to come, too, when she would be fighting other women for a man. But Wade was not just any man. She loved him dearly and wanted to keep him in her life.

Again, she said, "Well, he told me to come, and I have been with him this entire trip. He is mine."

They almost had a catfight, but security got between them. Later, after they finally left, Bella asked him about it, and he denied any such claims and believed them to be nonsense. He added, "But I would like a woman that would fight for me."

Whoa, love him for this or leave him for this. Bella, in her immaturity and blindness, thought it was love. She thought this is what real relationships look like, and she stayed – looking stupid.

A horrible, demon-infested man was prevalent at this point.

Wade would tell Bella to stop asking so many questions all the time. Tell her she was controlling because she needed to know everything all the time. She listened to him in quiet depression because she did not want to let him go, although every fiber of her being was screaming at her to run far away from that man.

She was in love with a demon and did not realize she was being sucked off her natural-born energy.

Chapter 2: The Break Up

Bella finally broke up with him and said she was done when he supposedly had his ex-girlfriend pregnant. She had texted Bella and told her that she was pregnant and that it was Wade's. Bella was willing to even accept this. Why? She was nineteen. No kids. Beautiful. No need to have this drama this young. All for the love of this boy. Ignorance. She wrote him a text saying how she was done with him. He could raise his baby with her and probably said a few more sweet things. Too sweet. But he did not reply, and she did not hear from him for a few weeks. Then he called crying and said he wanted to be with her and the baby was not his.

Well, for weeks, Bella knew he had also been talking to her because the ex-girlfriend had receipts honey. She had emailed Bella the text messages. The ex-girlfriend had emailed call logs and pictures she had taken with Wade on multiple occasions. Besides that, Bella had started talking to a new guy. He was sweet and wanted to travel with her and buy her things. She really liked him, but she gave into Wade after pleading during that phone call. The ex-girlfriend eventually had a miscarriage, and so the truth of that was never figured out... but he would never leave the Ex alone for good. Not ever. Bella did not understand and did not want to.

They couldn't stay away from each other, but mostly Bella just could not get enough of him. She loved him too much, and soon she realized she couldn't be without him. So they discussed moving in together. Bella was coming close to graduating in a year. She just wanted to be closer in hopes that maybe she could give him what was needed. So much so that he would not need anyone else. Up until this point, Bella had not met any of his family members. Wade would always say he was not ready for that.

After talking about moving in, he knew he would have to let her meet his family since he still lived with them, and Bella did not know that. Wade had been lying, saying that he had his own apartment. He has been living with his aunt and uncle since he was five. His mother left him when he was young, and his dad had another family, and he never claimed to be his dad in hopes that he would never have to explain it to his wife. His mother would constantly tell him that he was nothing when he was young. She would say she could not stand to look at him because his eyes looked like the devil, like his dad. When he turned five, his mom dropped him off at his grandparents and never came back.

His grandparents were pretty old, so they did the best they could, but his uncle knew Wade would need more as he grew, so he and his wife took him in. His uncle taught him how to do electrical work. As he grew, Wade got his own business with the security systems, but he had not been working any contracts. He told Bella that he had moved back in with his uncle and aunt to save up to buy a house soon. He then told her that he was in between contracts at the time, so he would not be able to really take care of her as she wanted. He had been getting money from his ex-girlfriend for everything. Bella said, "Well, what if I get a job and we go half on everything?"

Bella was hoping that would seal the deal. Wade said, "Okay. We can just stay at my aunt and uncle's house for a while, and then we will move when you graduate."

Bella was excited. Wade had convinced her to work part-time and move out of her dorm.

Bella found a job. She would work to save money, and Wade would ask her for money for different parts while working almost every week. Bella would give it to him, thinking that his business was taking off again, but Wade was taking his ex-girlfriend out, buying meals for other girls, and taking them on dates. He and Bella would smoke weed and eat and made the most embracing love. Little did she know that the clouds they blew were clouding her judgment of him. She loved a monster, but the fog did not let her see this.

He would take Bella to school and work and come back late to get her sometimes, and when she would ask him why he was late, he would say, "Don't worry about it. I mean, if you had your own car, you could take it yourself."

One day he popped up while she was working and brought flowers and a Hershey Bar for her. Bella had been feeling like things were on the rocks lately, but this gesture had her back in her feelings all over again. Wade said he had something planned for her when she got off. She was again excited. When she got off, he came and said, "I know things have been pretty difficult lately. I have not been the best man lately, and I apologize."

He pulled up to the house. There was a car there. He said, "Here you go, this is yours."

Bella couldn't believe it. She asked him where he got it from and how, and with what money. He said he had been able to get it for her and that it was in her name. Bella was speechless, but she said, "I can't afford the payments for this."

Wade became furious all of a sudden. He said, "You always ruining things thinking about the future instead of the present. You so ungrateful. This is why I don't do anything for you. I will pay for it. You always worried about money."

Again, Bella was left feeling hopeless. Feeling like she was wrong for thinking that he did not have a plan. She would think how dumb she was. Of course he had that figured out. Wade stormed into the house. Bella walked into the house. Wade's uncle was sitting at the kitchen table drinking some coffee. He asked Bella to sit down with him for a moment. Wade's uncle never really said much to Bella, but he had noticed the wrongdoing that was taking place.

He said, "Listen, you look hurt. I think you need to reach out to some family and find another place to go."

Bella said, "No, I'm okay."

Wade's uncle said, "Okay, but I will say. I love my nephew, but he isn't right."

Bella did not understand or did not want to. She went to her room and ran straight to the bathroom, and then sat on the toilet to think. Wade walked in and said, "I'm sorry. That was mean. If you want the car, you need to sign for it tomorrow at the bank. We can go together. It's your choice, but I will help you with the payments and insurance. I just don't want you to worry."

Bella could understand that. She said, "Yes, I would like the car, but I don't like how you talk to me. If you keep on, one day I will leave you."

Wade looked at her, bent down to get at eye level, and said, "You not going anywhere, and neither am I."

He gave her a kiss on the cheek and said, "Hurry up because I want you."

Bella thought to herself, "He loves me so much. I love the passion he has to keep us together."

She was so oblivious to the control and manipulation taking place.

The next few months were a struggle. School was a little challenging. And having to work, Bella did not have much time to study and stay up all night to pacify her boyfriend, who refused to study with her because he said she should be smart enough to not have to study so much.

Fall was coming to an end, and Bella wanted to visit her family for Christmas. Wade said he was not comfortable going that far away and said, "You shouldn't go either. So that you can work and save money."

But Bella needed to go. She missed her family, so she packed her bags and went to visit her family for Christmas that year. Bella was happy to be back. She hooked up with some friends from high school, and they went out. Her friends asked her how school was and how her relationship was. Bella showed pictures of her boyfriend and talked about his job and how much she loved him but refrained from revealing what she was really going through. While sitting at a restaurant, she noticed Anthony, a guy that was her high school sweetheart, before she left. He had a small baby with him, and he was by himself. She walked over to him and said hello. He got up and gave her a hug, and introduced Bella to his daughter. He asked her to sit for a minute. She didn't see a reason why not to. They talked and laughed and reminisced. He revealed that he had just had this baby with his baby mother, and she had died during childbirth, so he was learning this parenting thing all on his own. Bella encouraged him and told him he would be a great father. Anthony said, "Yea, I hope so. I always thought you would be the mother of my children." Bella blushed. She didn't understand why feelings seemed to be still there between them. She ignored them. She explained that she was in a relationship and hoped to have kids with him one day. Anthony said, "Well, he better treat you good. I hate that I lost the chance to keep you happy."

Bella hated it too.

Months passed with Bella and Wade trying to find an apartment. One day, she saw a text he had sent out to a friend talking about how he had been messing around with all these different girls and that he was 'kind of' in a relationship with Bella, but they were working on things. Mind you, this was soon after Christmas when she had bought him all these cute loving gifts, and he had been saying he wanted their own space together.

But looking back, there were plenty of times when he would tell her to get off him and push her away when she wanted to be all over him. Probably the guilt that he felt from cheating. Bella was angry, but she had nowhere to go, so she decided to keep it to herself until she graduated in a few months. Then she would move out back to Arkansas. Two weeks later, she let it go since he got her a bag of Bath and Body Works soap and lotion that she never even used and an apology that was not genuine at all. She thought history meant something, but she should have made him history.

One day when getting ready for class, Bella felt light-headed. She sat down for a bit, and the feeling left. She then got up and had to run to the toilet to vomit. She stayed home that day. She even started feeling like she had a cold. Her mother called, and Bella explained that she wasn't feeling her best, but she would be back up to get going the next day. Her mother asked her if she was pregnant.

Bella said, "No way, Mom. I just have a cold, and I ate some old pizza the other day."

This got Bella thinking, though. It could be. She had not taken a plan B in a while. She decided she would go to the store and buy a test. She came home and peed on the stick. She put it face down. Afraid of the answer. She waited and washed her hands and then turned it over, and she saw two lines. Bella could not believe it. She was excited and upset at the same time. She was worried about how Wade would react, especially how he had acted in the beginning. She waited for Wade to come back for lunch. He was surprised to find her at home. He said, "What's up. Why didn't you go to school??"

She said, "I didn't feel well."

She took out the pregnancy test and showed him.

He said, "I don't believe that."

Bella said, "Well, we can go to the doctor."

Bella called and went to the local health department, who confirmed she was indeed pregnant.

Wade acted happy about it in the office. He hugged her and kissed her stomach. As soon as they left, Wade asked, "Are you sure you want to keep it? We could get an abortion.

Bella said, "No. I will keep this baby."

Wade said, "Okay. I'll do all I can. I'll be a good father. I'll get whatever you guys need. You are family now."

He got everything they needed. They found a small apartment. It seemed like the baby was the change they needed. Bella was so disappointed that she was having her son without having all the money to care for him, but Wade made her feel like he would do everything he could to take care of all of them and that she wouldn't have to depend on her parents to help out since this was their child, and she wanted it to be all of their responsibility. They discussed how they wanted him to be raised. No cursing around him.

No smoking. Attend more church. He had said all those things were important to him.

Aaron was born. Everyone was happy. At that point, Bella had graduated. Wade's business was running better, and since the pregnancy started, Bella had not heard anything from the ex-girlfriend anymore, and Wade was being a positive person for the most part.

Aaron was beautiful. All she could think about was how much love she was going to give that little guy. How much joy she wanted him to have. His father even cried after he was born. He seemed like the number one dad.

Three weeks postpartum, Wade was getting anxious to have a night of passion again. He would say, "Don't you think it's time we do something yet. It's been like two months."

His sex clock was always far faster than Bella's. She was fearful of the pain that would occur when having sex again and possibly even getting pregnant again. But, she thought, well, I guess I better try, or he will be looking to get it elsewhere. Here started the no-love sex. The sex without passion. The I-have-to-do-it-for-you stuff. Misery at its finest.

It was a never-ending cycle of breaking up to make up to break up. It constantly had her in a state of walking on pins and needles and extremely high off lust. Bella didn't know he was testing her and just basically sucking the life out of her. She had gained weight, especially after having the baby, but Wade would say, "I love how you carry that weight," but later would say, "You are sloppy and fat, and you need to diet."

She was torn. When their son was six months old, he told her that she needed to move out because she came home with a honey bun he had seen at a client's house, and he was sure that Bella had been cheating on him. Bella had just started a new job and had no money saved to take her and the baby away. She pleaded with him and begged him to let them stay. He said, "Aaron would stay, but you have to go."

So she called the landlord and asked her to take her name off the lease and got as much of their stuff as she could, and moved out to Wade's aunt and uncle's house.

For a few months, they did the days and nights where they would swap having their son. He would call and say he was crying and that he could not get him to stop. It was hard, but life started getting better. Bella began walking and dieting with a co-worker, and things seemed like a breath of fresh air. Of course, her ex started to realize this, and honestly, all she really wanted was to find a way to put her family back together. She just wanted her son to have both of his parents by his side. But that still wouldn't be in the end. That family was just a façade.

So he started again with the messages of missing her. When Bella would drop her son off and pick him up, Wade would be talking about how he wanted his family back, but he had a whole woman staying with him already. Bella was just lost and still played the fool! BIG FOOL! She told him that she could not get back with him unless they were getting married. He proposed to her. It wasn't anything spectacular, but she had told him years before that she didn't need it to be, but she expected more with all they had been through.

Bella thought she should have said no, but realized she would do anything for her son. She had to try even though the vibe was off. This was no longer love. It was just work, and that's what her marriage would be.

She wanted to start planning the wedding immediately, but her fiancé had other hoops for Bella to jump through before jumping the broom. He would say, "I'm not ready to get married. I don't have enough money. You don't do enough for me. You don't talk enough. You don't cook enough." The list was ridiculous. He even had the audacity to say, "You should be glad I chose you. I could have had anybody."

It made her feel special, but it was just so ignorant. Ignoring facts! She let her emotions get the best of her. Whenever Bella would threaten to leave, he would cry and talk about how Aaron would grow up in separated homes.

How that is not good for him and how much he loves her and he is sorry. He would bring up all the stupid stuff from his childhood, which is why he acts how he does. Bella would bring that up in arguments. Saying, "I'm sorry your mommy didn't give you all that attention, but I can't do it either."

That was her choice. Bella could not understand or realize that Wade was a broken man. When he brought up his mom for things she did negatively, instead of making her accountable and not accepting her bullcrap, he was bound to have problems. He would make excuses for her all the time. Bella was a lover and grew up at peace. He was not used to that, and she thought she could teach him differently, but a person must want the change for it to happen.

One year went by from their engagement. Bella was tired of Wade, and they were actually going to call everything off, but one day she had a feeling that she might be pregnant. While working one day, Bella decided to stop by the store and bought a test and took while she was in the store. (II)! She was pregnant. Bella called Wade and told him she would be coming by because they needed to talk. He sat down and started talking about how they need to end this and let it be over with. She stopped him and said, "I'm pregnant." He took a moment and said, "We will just try to work this out."

So on with the circus act again.

Bella's fiancé was leaving for a two-week job that would be out of state. While gone, Bella had started paying more bills since moving back in. She was happy to pull more weight since starting her tech career, but she was ready to be married and helping her spouse. Not to mention she was pregnant with this boy's second child rearranging her body, mind, not living for God, doing everything she could, staying with him through all the fiascos he took her through, so there was no way she was about to add bill-paying mother of two and not spouse to this.

He finally returned home from his job. Bella was happy that he made it back and was ready to discuss the next part of their journey. One day on the way to work, they were talking as usual, and he asked did she remember to pay the light bill. Bella said, "Yes, and did you remember I need to be your wife soon?"

He laughed like she was playing. She was like, "No, for real. If I am paying bills and stuff, then I need to be your wife."

He laughed again and said that she was right. He told her to choose a date, so all things were made final at that point. She was jubilant that he had agreed. She went to work that day super excited and ready to get back to her fiancé that night.

Well, night fell, and Bella got off work. She called Wade. When he picked up, he was angry and said he wanted her to get all her stuff out of his house today. She was like, "Listen, I just got finished with an eight-hour shift, I'm pregnant, and I don't have the energy for this." She just hung up.

When Bella arrived at the apartment, her clothes were outside, the locks to the door had been changed. She tried to call, but Wade would not pick up. She got her things and went to Wade's uncle's house. Aaron was there with the aunt, thankfully. She got herself and the baby ready for bed, and they slept. The following day, Wade said he should not have to marry her because the girl he paid all the bills with wants to be married to pay bills.

Well, she would have already married you, so sorry, you just didn't want to get with the program."

She was perplexed. She hung up again. Bella had made up her mind to go back to Arkansas. He called later and left a voice mail saying, "Don't worry about coming back. I'm bringing your stuff. Some will be put in storage."

She was flabbergasted.

It all just didn't make sense to her. He came over to his uncle's house and was saying how sorry he was again. Wade said, "I didn't want you to go for real. I was just acting crazy and thought you had roots on me, so I put salt on everything, and now everything is okay."

"Roots!? I mean, that's what made you act this way?" Bella yelled. At the time, her hormones were all over the place. Again, she just wanted her family, so she did not even second guess them getting back together but looking back now, this was just another betrayal of herself. Should have followed her first mind.

Few months passed, and they moved out of that place and moved into a storage building room. A shed at best. They could not find anything else at the time. It was crazy that she did this, but Bella thought to herself, *he loves me,* and if she showed him, she would go through the toughest times with him, then for sure he would marry her. He would cook them dinners, and they would all eat together in that little room. Their son was very young that everything amused him. He didn't really notice the struggle.

Finally, one day they found a house in Bella's hometown, and they all decided to move back so that Aaron could get to know his grandparents better. Wade and Bella moved all of their things into the new place. They finally had a house to bring their new baby home to after the marriage.

Chapter 3: New Beginnings

The wedding was small but beautiful. Nothing she had ever dreamed or imagined which she loved. Her family, including his aunt and uncle, came together to celebrate their union. Bella was getting her makeup done by the makeup artist. After Bella got into her dress, she had a few moments to herself. At that moment, Bella felt she should not marry Wade. She knew it would not be a happy marriage. It wouldn't probably be as beautiful as she looked. Behind all the makeup and fake smiles, there was so much misery, but Bella just hoped things would get better for the sake of their kids. So, when the big question was asked, she said, *"I do."* Funnily enough, her head shook 'no' when she uttered the two life-changing words. She should have listened to her body cues, it was her body's last attempt at stopping her from making this mistake, but she ignored it. Wade and Bella danced and laughed. He said a whole lot of meaningful words to make everyone, including Bella, cry, but there was no truth behind those words. The worst part is, Bella knew that too.

Two weeks later, Bella got the news that their daughter would be arriving early. So, she started preparations, and two days later, their daughter was delivered. Oh, the joy to meet their daughter, Teara. She was so beautiful, and Bella had so much love for her. Thankfully, she had survived the surgery safe and sound. Teara and Bella went home, and a few days later, Wade came back home from work. He was complaining about some work stuff and groaned about quitting this contract. At the time, Bella loved having him at home. Since marriage, it seemed like God was on their side, so Bella told Wade that she had faith in God. Perhaps, he would find Wade a better contract for their family and that he should stay home for a little while until that contract comes. She couldn't be more wrong.

Subsequently, Wade quit his job, and they were okay. At first, they struggled a little bit, but they made ends meet. Wade decided that since Bella had been going to school for a while without paying more bills, they should switch roles for a while, and Bella would pay the bills while he finished school. She agreed to return that favor, but she wanted him to continue paying for the car note. Wade committed to pay the note. When Teara was about a month old, he was on the phone with someone involved in a heated discussion about the car payment. Long story short, Wade had not been making the car payments for months even though he had been working for months before that. Bella tried to convince the company by explaining their situation. She promised to make a payment as soon as she got back to work. In summary, the man told her, *"You are a nice woman, and honestly, I hate having to do this to you and your family, but your husband is very disrespectful, and I cannot sympathize with him for this."* All she could say was, *"Wow! Okay."* The car was repo-ed. This was just the beginning; the lies just kept coming. One Sunday, Bella's mother came over to visit with them and the baby. She had been with Bella and the kids all day. Dawn would feed the baby and play with Aaron and Teara. Wade came home after trying to make contracts and asked why Bella had left some chicken out of the refrigerator. She told him, *"I did not know I had left it out and that I did not mean to."* He said, *"If you are trying to say I need to eat, then that's all you have to say."* She was so confused at this point, so Bella laughed and tried to explain, *"No, I did not mean to leave it out."* Then, Wade got loud and made accusations about this chicken. He went as far as to claim that she was trying to poison him. Dawn was so upset that she decided to leave. She never stayed at Bella's house again. It was painful for her. He was doing too much, and Bella knew things were not going to last this way.

    Bella returned to work again. She and Wade worked out a schedule where he would watch the kids when he was not in school, and Bella's friend watched them on other days. The only thing of concern is, Bella did not have a car of her own, and her credit was so messed up that she could not get another one on her own. She set her schedule at work to go in at around 8 in order to drop off the kids at her friend's place on Wade's school days. Then, he would drop Bella off at work, go to school, and pick her up when she would get off. It worked for a while, and he wanted to start his own business with wiring and electronics. Being so happy to be a wife and make money, she decided to help her husband by getting a family vehicle that he could drive for his business. If he drove that one, then he would have his own car. She told herself, *"I would keep the payments up, and it would be in my name anyway, so no worries."* They found a nice SUV, and he was happy to be able to do more things he needed to do for his company. Bella asked her dad to sign with her, and she got the car. Bella did her best to encourage Wade, but he would always say she wasn't doing enough. He would be so upset that she didn't want to start a business of her own or something that he created for her. She only knew how to work hard, so it was hard for Bella to spend her time doing that. She tried to help with his ideas the best she could, but it was never enough. He made some money doing wiring for some small companies, but Wade wouldn't tell her everything. Neither did he show her most of the things in his junk room, AKA his office.

 They were in the same city, and he would be asking her to video call him to check if she was actually working, clocking in and clocking out. She even had to print out some timesheets. When it was time for him to graduate, the day of,

Wade told her not to come and see him walk. He needed to drive the SUV to take him and the kids to the graduation ceremony and later to a party with his friends. This hurt Bella because she couldn't even understand why she still showed up. She was proud to see him walk, so Bella went to Publix and bought a cake and balloons. She set up the restaurant for a celebration.

When he arrived, Bella was smiling and waiting with open arms despite everything that had happened that morning. He didn't even hug her and refused to smile for any pictures. He just said, *"Get out of my face, you demon."* An outrageous deception. She sucked it up. He made her so upset, but as his friends arrived and she prepared a meal for the kids, Bella smiled. Wade hugged and kissed them as if nothing was wrong. They all made it home. He told her soon after making it there that he was thankful for what she did and apologized for the way he acted. Bella blew her top that day and went straight off on him and cried her eyes out. He just looked at her and said, you need to stop stressing so much. He was driving her insane. She ended up going out with him later to a baseball game. It was a crazy toxic relationship.

She got her period when their daughter was about 5 months old. It was small and normal at first, but Bella got a period that never stopped for 1.5 years the following month.

She went to the doctor for a checkup and was told to lose weight because she was high risk for cancer. She said maybe if Bella got on birth control, it would help. She tried birth control after Aaron, and it would either give her fibroids or cause her to bleed for long amounts of time. Nothing helped her and Wade did not care. Irrespective of everything, lovemaking was a must no matter what Bella felt or how drained she was or how nasty she felt. He did not care. Wade had the audacity to tell her that she should be doing more. He was getting it every night, and she was bleeding every day. It was horrible.

To make matters worse, Wade told her other women could do more. Bella was paying for a vehicle that he was using. Giving him the goods every night despite everything going on. She was also working and taking care of the kids. He eventually got back to work because she was so drained with low iron. She could not work for a few weeks, but he paid half of the bills. Wade's old car, which Bella had been driving, stopped working. The next day, Bella had her mom drive her and the kids home. When he got home, he asked about the car, and Bella explained that it wasn't working before going on to ask for her car. He refused to give it to her. *"You are not getting it."* He mushed her. So, she got a spare key late at night, and he chased Bella outside. She drove the car away to her parents with no shoes and her nightclothes on. She needed her work clothes and kids at this point, so Bella had her parents take her back to the house crying and calling 911. By the time Bella called, she had learned that he had already called dispatch.

The police were already there when they arrived. They explained that since Bella purchased the car while they were married, he also owned it, and she had to bring it back. After the police finally left, Bernard said, *"Why are you crying Bella? It's going to be hard sometimes in marriage, but you both cannot be doing all of this."* When everyone was leaving, Wade called a friend, packed his stuff, and left. Bella still tried to get him to stay. He said he couldn't because he did not have a ride for work in the morning. Bella was going crazy thinking how ridiculous things had gotten. A few weeks later, he told Bella that he had been saving money for a divorce. Bella had been struggling to pay the bills while he would miss paying the water bill. This meant she would have to bathe the kids with water bottles while he saved money. She was so mad the next morning when he refused to give her the keys to the truck that she grabbed her window cutter and busted the windows out of the car so he could not drive. He ran out of the house to record her in action. This made her realize the way this relationship was making her act and how she was becoming the monster she married.

Chapter 4: The Kids

Later, they talked, and Bella thought they were on a new road. She was sadly mistaken, and the arguments continued. He complained that she did not talk to him enough. He needed Bella to stay awake throughout the night to talk to him while he was at work, or he would talk to other females. Bella was at a point in her life when she and her kids were all that mattered. She would check-in, and if the kids were happy and she was tired, then oh well. She would fall asleep, which made him upset. For the next year, she found herself growing out of this cycle.

Bella's coworker convinced her to do a water-only fast. The first day was the hardest, but things got easier later on. She thought this might also help with the bleeding, but it did not. Regardless, she ended up doing this fast for 7 days. During this fast, Bella felt like she had clearer thinking and clarity in the direction she was going. Bella knew if things did not change for her and Wade, she would leave him by the end of the year. They took a trip to Texas and had a good time with the kids. However, when they came back, Bella was still bleeding so much that she went to the hospital. They found nothing cancerous or any infections, but they gave her some pills to stop the bleeding. When she went to follow up the next week, her doctor explained that she would probably get her period back in two weeks. He cautioned her that it might be worse than before unless she got the Nexplanon in her arm. She was not comfortable with that but decided to get it anyway in hopes that she would not get pregnant before leaving this marriage. Her period did come back, but it was not as bad, and 7 days went by. She was so relieved. Wade and Bella had been working out and eating healthier. She was still not getting any rest from work and wound up staying up half the night, but things were better with Wade and the kids.

One Sunday, Wade left for the entire day. They had each other's location on their phone, so she looked to see where he was out of curiosity. She called him, but he didn't return her calls. He came back the next day stating he needed a break. *"You left the kids and me."* Bella yelled. It was met with silence. Then, one night when Bella was going to pay the rent, he came outside saying, *"I know you are going to have fun with your other man."* He took her ring off and threw it in the bushes. A few weeks later, he bought her another one. She was stupid enough to think that was cute and that it meant something.

Bella had put Teara to sleep, and Aaron wanted to stay up with Wade. He thought Bella was asleep, and she heard him on the phone with a woman. They were talking about sending pictures and everything. She was appalled, Bella got up and started taking his stuff outside. *"Yeah. Go be with her."* At that point, she knew the end was close. One moment, he asked her for money for his company, and in the next moment, he would ask her when she was moving out. Every day without fail, he would bring her a folder with divorce papers. They sat down to fill it out one day, and she just left. Bella and the kids went to stay with her parents and never went back. She was doing everything on her own with the kids, so it did not bother her. She got a second job and worked hard to get a place of their own. Wade asked her if she was done and whether they were coming back, to which she said no. Every day, he would constantly tell her, *"I'm going to have the police serve you the papers if you don't come to sign these papers."* Bella always told him she would not sign anything until an attorney looked things over. She stood her ground but got her things out of his house because he would threaten to take her things somewhere that she did not know. He threw her mail outside along with everything else. One night after getting off from work, she had made plans with her dad and a friend from work. She told Wade about dropping by to get her stuff and the kids' stuff with a U-Haul. He was gone and said he could not come because his girlfriend was sick. Bella said that she would call the police to meet her there and open it for her. He replied in an angry tone, *"I would be there."* When they got there in the middle of the rain, over half of her stuff and the kid's stuff was piled on the side of the road. He said, *"You will regret this."* Her dad was so upset, but he just kept his cool and said, *"She will be okay."* Her coworker, Kody, was mad, and he walked up to him and said, *"You should be ashamed of yourself. You are a nobody treating this special lady like this. When she divorces you, I will take care of her and your kids how it's meant to be."* Wade took a swing at Kody but missed and Kody hit him square in the jaw. Kody kept swinging until Bernard broke them up. Wade had a black eye and bled from the nose and mouth. Bella, her dad, and Kody hurried to finish getting what they needed while Wade threatened to sue all of them.

The next day, Bella and the kids moved into their new home. She got some furniture, and for the first time in a long time, everyone was happy. She filed for a divorce, and he was served. They did not communicate after that day except the one instance when he wanted to ask when he would get the kids. She started going out with friends again and began living a better life. Bella still wanted her family though, and it wasn't normal to be without him. Kody was there for her through it all and trying to comfort her. She picked up a new sewing habit and began drinking her pain away when the kids were not with her. They kept her going. They kept her happy and motivated, so she did her best to do the same thing for them during all this especially. Before the divorce was finalized, Bella and Wade began having marital relations again. Bella realized this was a big mistake. When they went for the final hearing, she told the judge that it had happened, but Bella still didn't want to stay married to Wade anymore. Subsequently, the divorce was finalized, and they continued to do things together. They claimed it was for the kids, and he would say our kids need to see us together. They came up with the family on Mondays, where they would play games and spend time together. One thing led to another, and they got back together but not entirely because Bella was not doing this for love, it was for her kids. She did not trust him at all.

Teara's doctor said that she needed to see a specialist about a small heart murmur. Wade wanted to come along for a two-hour drive. Bella said sure because even though they argued, she figured they should do this for their daughter. They met the doctor, who explained that surgery wasn't necessary; she could grow out of it, which relieved Bella. When they got in the car, she sighed in relief, *"Thank you, God."* Wade replied, *"I told you so. Why do you listen to those doctors anyway?"* Bella responded, *"Listen, let's just be thankful. Now, you just have to pay half for the doctor's visit and not a surgery."* A frustrated Wade insisted that he would not pay for that, and Bella should have just listened to him. He kept going on and on so far as to suggest that her fat self just wanted some money to eat. Bella stopped the car and demanded Wade get out and walk. He got out, and Bella drove off, but Teara started crying in the back seat. So, she turned around and picked him up. They had more nights of arguing and passion each day until she tried to stop because Bella did not want to end up pregnant again. It was too late.

The baby in her womb came all too quickly after the divorce, and when she took the test at his house, the first thing he said was, *"Who you been f**king with."*

"What?! You. You are the daddy as she had tears in her eyes." Bella did not want this for the baby. It was unfair.

Wade exclaimed, *"It will be fine. We will figure it out."*

The next week, he pressured Bella to tell her parents. She told Wade about her decision to wait because they kept the kids, and adding another child while Bella worked would not make them happy. Wade wouldn't show up consistently, and besides, his child would not make them happy at all. She told him that she was not ready, but he just didn't want her to have anyone else to lean on. He felt that if she moved back in with him, it would give him control again, but Bella refused to go through it again. He threatened to tell her parents, and they argued back and forth. She went to the doctor and got confirmation before telling her parents she was 6 weeks pregnant. Naturally, they were upset. It wasn't about her pregnancy, but because she had been with Wade.

Chapter 5: Time For Change

Learning that she was pregnant with the third child was devastating to Bella. To be able to carry a baby, she was so happy and willing, but to carry Wade's baby was not how she wanted her baby's book to start off. She misinterpreted this as a sign that they were meant to be together. Bella still didn't quite understand why at that time because she would always say, *"God, you just being funny because I was married to this man and wanted a baby during our marriage, but I never got pregnant. I bled almost the entire time being married to him. But this baby wants to come now."* Bella wanted to be a thot this year and hit the clubs. She wanted to do men how she had been done. This was the year she thought she would do what she wanted, but she got pregnant.

Wade said he wanted to stop working contracts in Arkansas and move to another state for better contracts. He wanted to stop the child support payments until he started his next contract. Bella explained that he could stop making child support payments for 1.5 months, but he would need to resume making his payments in some way to catch up. In hindsight, she was dumb for letting him have that freedom because she was still working and putting in so much more effort for the kids than he was.

Weeks went by with Wade abandoning them and he stopped keeping in touch with her or the kids. He moved out of state and did not call anyone. Bella texted him to ask for the money or a schedule for when he would return for the kids. She was met with silence until one morning when he texted Bella demanding she bring the kids to the park immediately or he would not be able to see them. He declared she had 15 minutes to get them there. Bella refused to do it because she was spotting that morning. She dropped them off with her mom and went to the doctor. He called the police and drove to her parent's house to get the kids without even informing Bella. Throughout this time, he would text her and threaten Bernard and or Bella by saying things like, you better hope nothing happens to you or your dad. He was furious that she would not agree to do everything he wanted her to, especially for the kids. Then, one day, when Bella let him come by the house to pick up the kids before work, she fell for him again. When people say strange addiction, this is what they mean. For the next few months, this man came in and out of Bella's home. He said he had a home in Florida now but stayed at Bella's house to take care of the kids during weekend visits and other days while she worked. One night while talking, he told Bella about another girl he got pregnant. It was unbelievable and insane. Bella felt like she was failing her kids. Each night, he would either call her evil or hateful. He remarked how sloppy and fat Bella was right in front of the kids. Later, he would claim it's not what he meant or that he would not do it again. To top it all off, he was not giving any child support. It was a mess, and Bella was a mess. He wanted to know how much money Bella was making at her job and where she worked at. Bella refused to share that information because he did not need to know. He kept saying if we are working on a family and putting us back together, he should know. Bella didn't change her mind, and she still refused to tell him. He left when she told him to clean up after himself or if she told him not to do something with the kids in her place. He would tell the kids that their mother doesn't let them do anything. He always tried to make Bella look like a bad parent. Yet, every day, when he was not around, the kids would be sure to tell her that she was the best mother in the world. She felt like striving to be the best.

Close to the baby's due date, they were still going through it, but Bella had made up her mind; she was going to make it work because they have 3 kids that need a good example. This relationship was anything but an example one should set for their kids. The day before she was going to have a C-section, Bella had a pre-op appointment. She asked him to go since he claimed Bella was cheating during her appointments without him. They were not even together, and Wade told the kids that he did not live with them. The receptionist was asking her some questions. When asked about her emergency contact, Bella said it was her mother, which prompted Wade to walk out. Later, when she confronted him, he stated, "You and your mama got everything under control."

Bella replies, *"My mom is always going to be my emergency contact. You will be here for the delivery."*

"Nah. Let me get the keys so I can go sleep in the car."

"No. since you are always saying something about me cheating, you are going to sit here during this appointment."

They continued to argue until he got so mad and started sweating. He was uneasy about how everybody looked at how she was acting. Then, he acted as if he was on a call from one of his odd jobs that he was working since he did not even have a full-time nor part-time job at the time. So he took Bella's vehicle and went to work while she went to the appointment by herself. Kody came to pick her up. Then, they picked up Aaron from Bella's mom. He was so mad when he saw she was in the restaurant waiting with Kody. Bella began to tell them how everything was supposed to go, and he said, *"No. I'm not going. Let your mama go."* They got to the house, and he started packing all his stuff from her house and said, *"Tomorrow, you can get your mama and take whoever is the daddy of that baby with you. It's probably Kody. You are a liar and a slick hoe."* He said this in front of Aaron. Bella responds, *"Well, you can keep your kids then."*

It was Teara's ballet day, and she had on an outfit that Bella's mom made for her. She did not want it to get messed up, so she decided to bring her to Wade after she changed Teara's clothes. He was not having that and tried to get her before Bella, but he did not have a car seat. So, Bella told him she would not release Teara to him without the car seat. He told Bella to keep her, and he'll have the car seat when he comes to get her later. Bella and Teara went to her mother's. She asked her mom to come to the surgery. Dawn didn't only agree to do it, but she was happy to be there. Wade called to meet her at the park with their daughter. She got there, and Aaron was asleep. He was trying to put him in the car seat in Bella's car when she pulled in. Bella asked, *"What are you doing?"*

"You are going to keep all these kids since you won't let me be there for the operation tomorrow." He tried to tear up the door on her car by yanking it. She tried to drive off, but he did not strap Aaron in, so he was standing up. Bella was going to strap Aaron in, but she knew Wade would be violent with her. He jumped in the car and continued asking whether he could come, but she declined. He came over to her side, and Bella locked the door. While in the back, he had unstrapped Teara. Teara got out of the car while Bella was

yelling at him to strap them in the car so they could leave. He said, *"Let me just get my kids."* He continued to say, *"You are going to get them and keep them since I can't be there."* Bella did not know what to do. Eventually, he asked her again, and she said no, again. He spat in her face twice and said that he accidentally sneezed. Bella started to cry, and she finally got her kids in the car after threatening to call the police. Before leaving, he said, *"I hope you just die on the table tomorrow."* She went home and finished packing before making plans for the kids while she was in the hospital. Later, she ended up calling the police to report the event so that she would have something in place to keep him from being able to come to the hospital. The police said there was nothing they could do because there was no physical evidence that he had spit on her and just informed the hospital to prevent him from coming in. Bella asked the hospital to keep her records sealed as if she was not there.

    Bella's daughter was delivered, and oh how beautiful she was. She could not believe Aria was here in her arms. She could not believe she had a baby inside of her this year, but Bella knew that Aria had saved her. All of her kids did. He still texted Bella the day of her birth, asking if he could come to see them and bring Bella some flowers. She didn't allow that, but Bella let him come back in again soon after they got home. She had to try even after he spat in her face. She wanted her daughter to have a chance at having a family. A father in her life, but she quickly realized that it would not work out once again. Bella still ended up having sex with him one last time. After her last postpartum checkup, she was not pregnant, and Bella decided never to have sex with him again. He planned to live in Florida for good. He was working on things for their family. This boy even asked her to take all three of their kids and live in a hotel while he worked on building contracts. Listen, Bella was not above struggling for the right man, but he was not led on the right path by God. She told him no, so he told their son that he would no longer be his dad since they would not be around. He was going to be a father to the kids from his other baby mother. Bella looked at her kids after the last episode of him claiming she was evil, hateful, lazy, and fat. All of that in front of her kids and having them cry as he left with his stuff. *"I won't do this to them anymore."*, and Bella stayed true to her word.

The rest of that year was filled with more of his antics. He tried to sabotage any normal life Bella tried to build for herself and the kids. Previously, he refused to pay her child support until he was legally inclined to pay child support. He texted her a day before she finally sent off the paperwork and said that there was no actual proof that he was the father of those kids. In the state of Arkansas, he was not obligated to make any payments for kids that did not have a paternity test. This is a man that likes to post kids on Facebook and get attention and not actually love the kids. Bella knew that at this point. When they went to court, he told the people they lived together and mailed himself a check to Bella's address without her knowledge. He paid nothing for nearly a year prior and then claimed he lived with them. He would not get the kids when he was supposed to, either. The list of things went on, and there were other court dates to follow. They were definitely enemies moving forward. She could not work with him and learned that the true battle was against a spiritual enemy attacking her life long before he arrived in the flesh. She learned to attack her flaws which she would constantly battle with prayers, the bible, and God each day. They say you attract what you are, and she was not completely *right* when they met each other.

Bella recognized the parts of her that reminded her of Wade and decided to face those parts of her head on. When she and Kody made things official, her life was whole once again. They would take the kids to church, play games together, and date each other. After they married, they conceived another beautiful child, and Bella could not be happier. As for Wade, he would text and say rude things, but he was eventually blocked from Bella's phone. He was only allowed to text Kody, so he didn't text at all. The kids missed their dad every now and again asking about him, but they were happy to have Kody play the role of a father for them.

Bella loved Wade. She wanted to have his last name without understanding that it was not about the name; it was about the soul. She thought if she loved him enough, they could make it work. If she let him get the anger out, maybe Wade would eventually treat her better, but Bella decided to stop being a punching bag for his childhood issues. She wished the best for Wade and prayed for his salvation. James 4:7, *"Be subject therefore unto God; but resist the devil, and he shall flee from you."*

www.ingramcontent.com/pod-product-compliance
Lightning Source LLC
Chambersburg PA
CBHW071757080526
44588CB00013B/2275